A HEALING JOURNEY

Poems of Faith, Healing, Recovery, and Coping with Grief

Stephon C. Void

South Carolina United Methodist Advocate Press

Copyright © 2023 by South Carolina United Methodist Advocate Press

All rights reserved. No part of this book may be reproduced or transmitted in any form or by any means, electronic or mechanical, including photocopying, recording or by any information storage and retrieval system, without permission in writing from the Publisher.

First published in the United States of America in 2023 by the South Carolina United Methodist Advocate Press.

Library of Congress Cataloging-in-Publication Data
A Healing Journey
p. cm.

Cover: Florin Cristian Ailene

ISBN 979-8-9851495-8-6

Praise for *A Healing Journey*

"Stephon Void has penned the poems that we all need in our time of collective grief and anxiety. He approaches grief with a reverence and sensitivity that reminds us that grief is an unavoidable part of life on planet earth. Especially now. Thank you, Stephon. This is the book that we have needed."
—Dr. Safiyah Fosua, DMin Track Professor of Black Theology & Womanist Theology, Nazarene Theological Seminary

"Through the artistic writings of poetry, Stephon Void stirs our emotions. He remembers his father's journey through the last days and months of his life. But there's more. His father's journeying becomes part of his family's journey, Stephon's personal journey. We are invited to know God as a healer of broken hearts and lives. Further, the journey of life is a miracle because we do not walk this way alone. God is with us. We therefore come to understand that in all circumstances of life, God's love and grace abound. A beautiful work!"
—Rev. Janice L. Frederick-Watts, ordained elder, South Carolina Conference of The United Methodist Church

"Mr. Stephon C. Void has done it again. *A Healing Journey* does not disappoint. This thought-provoking memoir of poems depicting daily occurrences in one's life has me rethinking how I approach life's difficult moments, those life-altering decisions, and the simple joys I find in my own life. The subtle ways he causes you to always refer to the love of God through grace is a blessed reminder of his strength and faith in the Lord. To know Stephon Void is to love him. Reading his work opens you up to a re-examination of how we approach life's difficult moments and joys. Job well done, my friend. Job well done."
—Rev. Sheri Yvette-Base White, ordained elder and pastor of New Covenant United Methodist Church, Bowman

*This book is dedicated to my dad, Carlisle Void. This book was supposed to be a gift for you once you were cancer-free. Now it's to honor your journey and transition to your heavenly rest.
It's also dedicated to my mom, Shirlene Void.
Your dedication to Dad and myself has not been forgotten.
Aunt Queen Ester, your support during this past year has been a blessing. Last and certainly not least, it is dedicated to all health-care professionals who sacrifice their lives for the sake of others.
Without your God-given gifts,
we cannot reach our fullest potential.*

Table of Contents

A Letter to My Readers 9
The Fist Bump...11
I Pray that I'll Be Ready..13
Oh, You're So Strong...15
Another Waiting Room 17
Remember, I'll Be with You...19
Get Up..21
Tears in Babylon...23
Paid in Full...25
Made in My Image 27
I Need You 31
Caregiver's Prayer 33
With Every Breath...35
Silence 37
Instead 39
I Long for the Day 41
How to Mend a Broken Heart.......................................43
We Will Get Up..45
One More River to Cross 47
We Stand on Giant Shoulders 49
There's No Quit in You 51
Waymaker, Chain Breaker 53
Someone 55
Another..57
Wear It Well 59
Give Me Strength 61
Remember..63
Take a Breath 65
Do You Know 67
Compass 69
Autopilot..71

Faith	73
The Sending Forth	75
Mess	77
Whose Hands You're In	79
With Every Drop	81
He Carries Me	83
One More	85
Faith over Fear	87
It's OK, Momma	89
Sick	91
The Fist Bump Part II	93
When My Time Comes	95
My Dad, My Hero, My Friend	97
Three Pairs	99
Another Restless Night	101
No Worries	103
Six Stars	105
There's No Road Map for Grief	107
A Letter to Dad	109
Cherish	111
About the Author	113

✝

A Letter to My Readers

To those of you who read my first book, welcome back. To my new readers, welcome to the journey. I thank all of you for supporting this new project. I hope it touches and inspires you in a special way.

Some of you may ask, "Why did I want to publish so soon after writing the first book?" Well, the first book only told a portion of my story. For the past thirty-nine years of my life, I have suffered from complications of a rare disorder called Kartagener's syndrome. It's a form of another disorder called primary ciliary dyskinesia. It occurs in one out of every thirty thousand births in the world. It's so rare I know of only one other person in South Carolina who has it. My cilia don't work properly, and that has led to many setbacks. I have had five sinus surgeries, countless ear tube placements, and I constantly fight to have healthy lungs. I have had infections that have been so severe I had to have intravenous antibiotics twice.

The one constant throughout all of it was my unwavering faith in God. He has kept me through it all. This illness inspired my faith to be strong, and it also influenced my professional career to be in the sciences. I've used it as a testimony and a stepping stone. I have written about my struggles with all the tests and clinical trials and placed them in this body of work. Also included are some writings that shine light on issues important to me. Some are issues of faith and how we express it; others are race and, once again, social justice.

The second catalyst for this book is the journey of my dad, Carlisle, and his eventual passing because of complications from cancer. Two months prior to my first book's release, he was told he had Stage Four head and neck cancer. He needed surgery and, following that, six weeks of chemotherapy with radiation. Some of the writings are like a journey—from his first surgery to his second surgery and, sadly, his passing. The first poem, "The Fist Bump," was from his first surgery, which was October 26, 2021.

My dad went on life support on May 25, 2022, after fighting sepsis and pneumonia. I told him this book was for him and gave him our last fist bump. On May 26, 2022, he transitioned to the Church Triumphant.

Toward the end, you will find "The Fist Bump Part II" in his honor. It's like a bookend to his seven-month battle with cancer.

My last book was a personal challenge. This one was a personal journey. I hope it gives you some insight on me as a patient, caregiver, son, and follower of Christ. I also hope my words cause you to do a little soul-searching and self-reflection.

Thank you for taking this journey with me.

—Stephon Void
March 2023

The Fist Bump

When we think of a simple gesture
like a first bump
a few things come to mind.
It could be the famous double-fist that the Obamas did.
To them it meant, "Yeah, baby, we did it. We made it to the White House."
Maybe you see ballplayers on the court or field bump fists after a big play.
Friends do it to say "hi" or "what's up."
It's endearing.
It's powerful.
It's encouraging.

Moments ago, a fist bump between me and my dad was more than that.
It was a confirmation that we will see each other on the other side of his surgery.
That meeting of hands meant
I love you.
I got you.
God's got you.
It meant I'll take care of you.
I'll take care of Mom.
Everything is going to be fine.

With a tap of our hands, the angels took over your care
And God set his plan in motion.

Dad, the next time we bump fists
it will be in the celebration of your healing.
It will mean it is time to take you home.
You get to sit in your favorite spot.
It will mean we beat this thing.

I Pray That I'll Be Ready

Lord, I pray that I'll be ready
Ready for the blessings
Ready for the calling
Ready for what lies ahead

Lord, I pray that I'll be ready
Ready for the long days
Ready for the sleepless nights
Ready for the hard work

Lord, I pray that I'll be ready
Ready for doubters
Ready for the plotters
Ready for the evil the lurks at every turn

Lord, I pray that I'll be ready
Ready for that new opportunity
Ready for that new relationship
Ready to navigate unknown horizons

Lord, I pray that I'll be ready
Ready for when my dreams become reality
Ready to lead
Ready to follow

Lord, I pray that I'll be ready
Ready to be patient

Ready to listen
Read to learn

Lord, help me to be ready
Ready to live
Ready for the everlasting
Ready for it all

Oh, You're So Strong

People always say "Oh, you're so strong"
They don't really know how expensive that strength is
This strength cost two hours a day doing breathing treatments
It costs hundreds of thousands of dollars on antibiotics, procedures, and medicine
You don't know how much time I sit in waiting rooms to see doctors
To hear more bad news
It costs me pain to get to a place just to hear like a normal person
I must tell the people I care about the most "no" because I can't physically do anything sometimes
The price is feeling lonely or like you're missing out
The prayers …
The tears …
The albuterol- and prednisone-induced sleepless nights …
My strength comes at a price—
A price that was paid for by the blood of a sinless lamb
It's coming from every lash of the whip and every rip in his flesh
I'm strong because of the redeeming love of the risen Christ
When you see me standing tall it's because I gain my strength from God's love
That's what keeps me pressing forward
That's what holds me up
That's why I am so strong

Another Waiting Room

Here I am in another waiting room
I got this huge clipboard with all the stuff
HIPPA form ... done
New patient profile ... done
Medical release form ... all done
Did they give me back my ID and insurance card?
Yeah, I see them now
Now I wait
Do I look at the next contest on The Price is Right?
Or do I read an article?
You know what ... I'll just say a little prayer
Whatever awaits me at the end of this, I can handle it
My strength and help come from God
He didn't bring me this far just to leave me alone
This is just another page in my testimony
It's another step toward victory
No matter the news I win
I win because of who I belong to
I win because the healing began before I took my first breath
It began when Jesus stayed on the cross
It began when he took on all the pain of the world on his
    shoulders
So today I will walk in the exam room with my head held high
OK, doc, I'm ready

Remember, I'll Be with You

My child, remember this
Throughout your diagnosis I will be with you
During every appointment
During every scan
During every surgery
I will be with you

When the first drops of chemo enter your veins
When the first particle of radiation hits your skin
When your nausea starts
I will be with you

When your weight changes
When your hair thins
When you feel tired
I will be with you

When you feel like you want to cry
When you get weak
When you question me why I allowed this
I will be with you

I was with you since your first breath
I know you from the crown of your head to the soles of your feet
I made you in my image
I saw every accomplishment
I saw your very first moments

I saw you through your failures
I was with you for every good day
I kept you during your worst days
I comfort you during every moment of grief

So as this new challenge arises,
Remember, my child
I will be with you
No matter the outcome
I will be with you
I will be with you always

Get Up

Get up
No! No! No!
Get up
I know how you are feeling
You're tired, right
The bed feels so great
All of the troubles are on pause if you stay in bed
Nope, not today, get up
You're anxious
You're having a flare-up
If you just lay here, you can deal with it tomorrow
Sorry, but get up
You can't let your fear win
You can't let your medical condition hold you back
Face it head on
Get up, get on up
Pray
Read his Word
Shower and prove the world wrong
Prove yourself wrong
Get up, shake it off, and get up
The victory has already been won
The ransom has been paid
You are healed and free because Christ said so
Get up
Because he got up out of the grave

Get up
Because the world needs your presence and your gifts
You got this

Tears in Babylon

Lord, your children are crying in Babylon
There are mothers, fathers, daughters, and sons crying rivers of
 tears
Flowing in Babylon
We are the diaspora
Taken from the motherland
Forced to build a nation with our bloody and battered bodies
They took our names
They separated us from our families
They stripped us of our identities

Lord, your children are weeping in Babylon
Mothers, fathers, daughters, and sons are crying rivers of tears in
 Babylon
We fought for freedom and equity and acceptance
We even gave our lives for it
The more we built, the more they destroyed
The more we created and innovated, the more they stole
The more we showed love, they turned it to hate

Lord, your children are wailing in Babylon
Mothers, fathers, daughters, and sons are crying rivers of tears in
 Babylon
We are killing each other to escape poverty's grasp
We are fighting over streets and turfs we don't own
We are leaving our children to fight on their own
The men and women who were called to serve and protect are

constantly putting knees on our neck
God, can we please get the targets off our back?

Lord, your children are hollering in Babylon
Mothers, fathers, daughters, and sons are crying rivers of tears in Babylon
We are stuck in an endless loop like crabs in a barrel
One child climbs, the other child is yanking him back
Instead of self-love we are preaching self-hate
Five hundred years and we still don't fully own our freedom, nor can we fully realize our dream
We are dependent on you, oh Lord, to remove the pain of our souls
Help us to overcome all the stumbling blocks that have hindered our way
Help all to see there is a brighter day coming.

Lord, your children grow weary in Babylon
Mothers, fathers, daughters, and sons are drowning in their own tears in Babylon

Paid in Full

I was sick.
I mean really sick.
It seemed like nothing that I did would help my condition.
So, I made my way to the clinic.
This clinic was a special one.
I didn't have to leave home.
It's open twenty-four hours and seven days a week.
Here is the shocker
There is no wait time to see the doctor.
All I had to do was call him.
He is known worldwide.
Some call him Emmanuel
Some say he is the Prince of Peace.
Others call him Yeshua.
I call him Dr. Jesus.
I said, "Hey, Jesus it's me again."
He walked in the room and sat next to me.
I told him about all that I was experiencing.
He didn't rush me. He barely even spoke a word.
He looked over his notes and patted me on the shoulder.
Then he took out his prescription pad.
He wrote a prescription out on the pad.
It said, "Read the following daily:
Mark 5:34
1 Peter 2:24
Isaiah 41:10
Jeremiah 33:6"

He said, "Don't worry my friend. I will take care of you.
Follow my directions, and my colleague the Holy Spirit will visit you regularly.
He and I will help you see the right people.
I know some good people, and I have equipped them to help you."
He shook my hand and I noticed the scar in the middle.
He walked out the door and
No bill was handed to me.
All that was left on my bed was a note that said, "All bills are paid in full by the blood of the lamb that was slain on Calvary. Go in peace and refer others to see the Doctor."
What a joy it is to know that Jesus paid it all for me.

Made in My Image

My child, I created you in my image
I gave you a mind not only to think and process information
I want you to use it to better the gifts I gave you
I want you to use it to think of others more than yourself
I want you to develop empathy for your fellow man
I want you to have compassion and wisdom
Use your mind wisely
Don't become so distracted that you miss out on life
Don't use anything to cloud it and inhibit its growth

I gave you your eyes
Yes, they help you to see the beautiful world
I want you to use them to see the humanity in others
Use them to see the needs of your community
Use them to appreciate these different cultures that your brothers and sisters have
Stop using them to compare others based on their clothing or skin tone
Use them to see me in others
Use your vision to make the world better for those who come behind you

I gave you ears to hear the beautiful sounds
Also use them to hear the cries of others
Use them to tune into my voice
Don't pollute your ears with gossip or slander
Don't clog them with hate speech or lies

Use them to discern what is right and just

I gave you a mouth
Yes, you can use it to communicate and taste the wonderful cuisine I have provided
Use it to be my voice in the darkness
Use it to sing praises and offer prayers
Use it to tell my story and your story
Never use it to tear someone down
Use it to offer thanks, praise, and worship
Use it to build others up
Use it to defend the voiceless
Use it to bring one another together
Stop using it to divide and cause confusion
Your voice is powerful
Whatever you profess can come to pass

I gave you your hands to touch and feel
I gave you them to build and create
Use them to lift your fallen brothers and sisters
Use them to cultivate and build on the vision I gave you
Use them to protect those who can't protect themselves
Use them to feed
Use them to give
Use them to comfort and embrace
Use them to build meaningful foundations for others to stand and build on

I gave you your legs to stand and to travel the world
Use them to go places that make you feel uncomfortable
Use them to stand on the truth
Use them to stand tall with confidence
Use them to kick open doors of opportunity for others
Use them to help push and pull those who have given up

Most importantly, I gave you a heart
Yes, it pumps life throughout the body
It's also the home to your soul
It's the seed of your emotions
If you trust me with it
I promise you that all I ask of you will become easier

My child, you are my reflection of me because I made you that way
You are precious to me
Cherish the life I gave you
And use it to make it better while you can

I Need You

Lord, I need you.
I don't need another doctor giving me bad news.
I don't need another test or scan.
I'm sick and tired of these tubes and needles.
I'm thankful for health-care but
Lord, give me some time with you.

I don't want to have another sympathetic card or phone call.
I don't need a cute photo sent to me from Pinterest.
If I hear someone say, "I'm praying for you," I'm going to scream.
I love my support system and all that they do, but
Lord, right now, in this moment, I need some time with you.

Lord, I need you to quiet the noise in my mind.
It's racing, thinking of all the things that can go right or wrong.
I need you to strengthen my resolve as I fight for my earthly life.
I need you to help me prepare for my eternal life as well.
I know that you are with me
But for just a few moments, give me you.

Caregiver's Prayer

Heavenly Father,
Thank you for the opportunity to take care of my loved one.
Thank you for keeping them
And providing me with the ability to be their helper.

As we embark upon and embrace this journey together,
Give us patience with each other.
There will be times that we will get frustrated and upset.
It's because we both remember when the roles were reversed.
They provided for me
And now it's my turn to provide for them.
Continue to grant me a kind and loving spirit.
Toughen my skin when they say something that they don't mean.
Give me an attentive ear to listen for what they may need.
Provide for us the means to afford the care that they need.
Grant me the strength to carry their load
And the wisdom to know when to let you carry it for the both of us.

Strengthen my heart as I see my once-strong warrior in their newly fragile state.
Remove any feelings of fear, doubt, and anxiety
As we weather this storm together.

Help me to always greet them with a smile
And may the only tears they see me cry
Be tears of joy.

Father, help me to make the best choice when it comes to their health and overall quality of life.
If this is for a little while or if this is our new normal,
Help us to be content with the journey ahead.
Father, I know that you are with us,
And we are looking forward to developing a stronger relationship with you.
In your name I pray,
Amen

With Every Breath

With every breath
Lord, I will praise you
I shout your name unto the world
My lips will always have words of thanks
I will sing songs to share my love for you
I will shout for joy.

With every breath
I will serve
I will show the world the power of your love
I will help others carry their burdens
I will go wherever you send me.

With every breath
I will witness
I will tell my story
I will share your good news
I will proclaim your goodness.

With every breath
I will build your kingdom
I will be a reflection of your light
I will be a living example of your love.

Until my last breath I will serve you.

Silence

The silence is deafening.
Lord, I can't hear your voice.
How do I even know you are listening?
How do I know that you care?

I sat here watching and waiting on you and I got nothing.
How can I know what to do if you don't lead me?
I'm lost like a ship without a sail at sea.
Why are you silent, Lord?
Father, I need you!

The silence is sickening.
Is this a test of faith?
Is there a lesson to be learned?
I know you are there, Lord!
God, please speak to me.

Your voice is calming.
Your voice is powerful.
Your voice is all I need.

I will not move.
I will continue to read your Word.
I will continue to pray until I run out of words.
I will wait until you speak.

Instead

Instead of a closed fist, offer a helping hand
Instead of noticing what makes us different, focus on what makes us similar
Instead of saying hateful words, offer words of encouragement
Instead of living in fear, live with great expectations
Instead of manipulating the game, make it fair for all to play
Instead of worrying, spend time in prayer
Instead of violence, choose peace
Instead of building walls, build bridges
Instead of being exclusive, be more inclusive
Instead of clinging to God's Word, live it and share it with others
Instead of hiding behind the four walls, see the community as your parish
Instead of being safe, take a leap of faith
Instead of longing for yesterday's glory, embrace the new day ahead
Instead of keeping God in a box, open it and see new possibilities
Instead of saying "we can't," say "yes, we can"
Instead of being just OK, focus on how you can be great
Instead of just seeing only the sin, embrace the heart of the sinner
Instead of pretending to answer the call, do what you are called to do
Be my church

I Long for the Day

Lord, I long for the day that we put the guns down
When mothers no longer cry as their child's blood soaks the street
That we build up our communities instead of tearing them down
That we fight for unity instead of turf and colors
That children no longer have active shooter drills.

Lord, I long for day that we regain our empathy
Police can see themselves in the people they are sworn to protect
Civic leaders will care more about the truth instead of how they
    win the next election
People will hear the cries of those who suffer alone.

Lord, I long for the day that the church is united
We can stand on truth and help those find it
We can shine your light of love in the dark places
Where we will no longer find ways to shun those who are
    different
Where we will open our hearts to a new vision.

I long for a better tomorrow
Where no child is cold or hungry
Where no one should be bankrupt to get health-care
Where no senior citizen should worry about being alone.

Until that day comes, I will pray
While I pray, I will work
While I work, I will witness

While I witness, I hope
I will do my part to make our tomorrows
Better than our yesterdays.

How to Mend a Broken Heart

How can you mend a heart that is broken?
A heart that is torn apart by a senseless act of violence.
A heart ripped in two by the loss of someone you loved dearly.
A heart filled with questions of "Why this, why now, and why it had to be them?"
A heart longing for understanding.
A heart yearning to see that person one more time.
Jeremiah, the prophet, said he saw a vision one day of a potter repairing broken vessels.
God revealed how he would restore Israel.
Just like Jeremiah's vision came to the past then,
It surely will happen again now.
God, the potter, can mend our broken hearts.
He's molding us in the hollows of his hands.
With every turn of his wheel, he's offering hope, peace, love, and restoration.
We can't mend a broken heart
But there is a God who can do that and more.

We Will Get Up

You take us from our homeland
You pack us tighter than sardines on ships
You take our names
You sell us like cattle
No matter how hard you knock us down
We still get up

You worked us from dusk until dawn
Fed us scraps
Separated our families
Tried to keep us ignorant of how powerful we are
You can whip us down,
But we will get up

We became free and tried to make a name for ourselves
You denied our patents and made them your own
You destroyed our communities to build lakes and parks
You tried to keep us separate and never equal
You made us guess how many bubbles are in a bar of soap just so
 we couldn't vote
You gave us books that washed away the truth
You can push us down, but we will get up

We marched for freedom
You burned crosses and sent water hoses and dogs
We sat for equality
You called us names

Martin had a dream and Malcolm wouldn't give up without a fight
You shot them down
You may intimidate us,
But we will get up

Now you use redlining, gerrymandering, and gaslighting to keep us in line
Now murder-by-cop and stand-your-ground laws are your new tools to thin the herd
Mass incarceration is the new slavery
Critical race theory and affirmative action are your new dog whistles
Guess what—you can strike us down and every time
We will get up

We will stand tall
We will educate ourselves
We will build strong foundations for the future
We will go high while you continue to go low
We will keep getting up

One More River to Cross

One more river to cross
Another battle to fight
God, help us cross
Help us to be all right

Another surgery, another test
Another trip unknown
One more time a tumor has grown
God, help the surgeon do their best

One more river to cross
Another battle to fight
God, help us to cross
Help us to be all right

One more day in a cold room
Another gown, another IV
Lord, help me obtain victory
Lord, may this part of my journey end soon

One more river to cross
Another battle to fight
God, guide us over
Help us to be all right

When this battle is over another begins
Radiation on my skin, chemo in my veins

Lord, comfort me through the pain
I know you've fixed it before and that you will do it again

One more river to cross
Another battle to fight
God, help us to cross
Help us to be all right

God, encourage my family and friends as they pray
Give them all the strength they need
As they wait for news throughout the day

One more river to cross
Another battle to fight
God, help us to cross
Help us to be all right

We Stand on Giant Shoulders

From the lands of West Africa
To the shores of the American colonies
Our ancestors dreamed and prayed for a better day.
While they worked from sunup to sundown
Facing torture and pain, they prayed and dreamed of a better day.
As they ran and hid in the darkness pressing toward freedom,
They prayed for a better day.
While witnessing a war for unity of our nation
They prayed for a better day.
As they saw crosses burning and towns they built destroyed by hate,
They prayed for a better day.
As they marched, boycotted, staged sit-ins
As they were beaten, hosed, and bitten by dogs
They prayed for a better day.
As they heard slurs and were escorted by the national guardsmen to integrate schools
As they endured jobs that kept them down
They prayed for better days.

Here we are today, standing on those prayers and actions
We are who we are because of their unwavering hope
They never gave up because they knew that we are next
We are the here and now

We stand on the shoulders of giants
There is no quit in us

There is no turning back
We have work to do
We have no excuse
We must continue to build on the legacy that paved the way
    toward the goal of freedom
Freedom for every human being
Freedom in every aspect of life
Freedom from the mentality of mediocrity
Freedom from self-hate
Freedom from spiritual depression

We stand on the shoulders of giants
They need us to wake up and build on the foundation they laid
So that one day our children can be able to stand on our shoulders
In a better tomorrow.

There's No Quit in You

I created you in my image
Nothing I make is junk or damaged goods
I gave everything you need to succeed
There is no quit in you

With a rod, I parted the sea
With a sling and a stone, I slew a giant
With one prayer I stopped the rain from falling
That power is also in you
So don't quit now

With the hem of a garment, I cured a woman
With clay, I healed a blind man
With three words I calmed a raging sea
That power is also in you
Don't you dare quit now

I fed thousands with two fish and five loaves of bread
I made a bridge out of water
In three days, I conquered sin and death
Deeply rooted in your soul is that same power
Don't throw in the towel now

Grief will not win
Hate will not overcome my love
Chaos can't touch my peace
Sadness will not defeat my joy

Illness will not overwhelm my healing
Depression has nothing on my gift of happiness
If you are in my care I will provide
Just trust in me and I'll do the rest

So don't give up now
The word "quit" does not exist in you

Waymaker, Chain Breaker

Waymaker, chain breaker
You've done it before
Do it again for me

Open another door
Be my bridge over the waters
Calm another raging sea

Waymaker, chain breaker
You've done it before
Do it again for me

Fill in another void
Heal this pain
Give me clear vision when I can't see

Waymaker, chain breaker
You've done it before
Do it again for me

Brighten up my cloudy day
Comfort me in my loneliness
Replace my sadness with glee

Waymaker, chain breaker
You've done it before
Do it again for me

Break the chains of doubt and depression
Break the chains of anxiety and stress
Lord, set me free

Waymaker, chain breaker
You've done it before
Do it again for me

Someone

Someone needs your story.
Keep writing it.
Someone needs your song.
Keep singing and playing it.
Someone needs your testimony.
Keep telling it.
Someone needs your sermon.
So, keep on preaching it.
Someone needs your love.
Keep sharing it.
Someone needs your skills.
Keep using them.
Someone needs your presence.
Keep shining your light.
Someone needs that precious smile.
Keep on smiling.
Someone somewhere is happy you are alive.
Keep on living.

Another

Another period of partial deafness
Another hope and prayer that it goes away
Another visit
Another waiting room
Another step on the scale
Another vitals check
Another session of explaining how my hearing has faded in one or both of my ears
Another fancy chair
Another tube gone
Another tube placed
Another slice of hope that this time it lasts
Another call to let everyone know I'm fine
Another prayer on the way home
Another chapter is written to tell my story and God's story
Just another moment as a Rare Disease Club member.

Wear It Well

You say "I wear it well"
Come and sit with me for a spell
I have a story to tell

You weren't there when I fell
Fell into my hell
When I needed God's grace
Just to show my face

Every day was filled with pain
All I saw was rain
Pain, rain, death, and sorrow
I had no hope for a better tomorrow

Living my life check to check
The storms kept coming, I was a wreck
To be honest it took a while
Before I was able to smile

Then I heard a voice that said "Take a look"
"My child, take a look in my book"
I began to read, and I began to see
All the promises God had for me

His plans on how to cope, grow, and succeed
All I had to do was listen, understand, and take heed
I gave him my life and I began to grow

I don't let my problems bother me anymore

There are times when I still cry
But I know crying only lasts at night, and daylight is nigh
I give my heavy loads to Jesus because he's strong
With him beside me, my trouble won't last long

I carry my problems well because he is my friend
I know I can depend on him until the end
Ever since I met him, I've never been the same
And I know I can do all things but fail in Jesus's name

Give Me Strength

Lord, give me the strength to fight
Everywhere I turn
Everywhere I look
There's something pushing back at me
It's always another no, or not right now
The very people I'm trying to pull up
Are trying to pull me down
There's always someone envious
But they understand how hard it took to make it
There's always someone ready to fire off negativity
No matter how much change I make
It seems like it's not enough
It's to the point that I'm tired
There are moments when I want to throw in the towel
It feels like the tears are flowing like rivers
Then I remember in your Word that you will never leave nor forsake me
It says when I am weak you are strong
I don't have to fight alone
You are in my corner
You have my back
You are there to push me beyond my limits
I can hold my head up high
I can fight the good fight
I can hold on to the final bell
I can declare victory
I can be free

Remember

Remember who you are
You are not your flaws
You are not your mistakes
You are not your failures
You are not your fears
You are not your doubts
You are not your illness or disease
You are not your addictions
You are not your past
You are not weak
You are not your sadness

Remember who you are
You are blessed
You are favored
You are redeemed
You are healed
You are restored
You are strong
You are an overcomer
You are accomplished
You are valued
You are loved
You are a builder
You are gifted
You are a child of God
You are everything He says you are

Take a Breath

Hey, wait for a second and take a breath.
Breathe in and breathe out.
It's something so simple.
We do it seventy thousand times a day.
If we don't do it, we die.
So every breath we take is a gift.
It's an opportunity.
It's a chance.
So what do we do with this gift?
Do we thank God?
Do we love our neighbors?
Do we help those who can never pay us back?
Do we uplift each other?
Do we worship God?
Do we take time out to tell someone, "I love you"?
Are we leaving the world a better place than we found it?
Do we take a break for ourselves to recharge?
Do we stand still long enough to hear God's voice?
Are we living in the calling he has on our lives?
Each breath we take is one step closer to our last breath.
Time is fleeing from us with every breath we take.
So what are we going to do with the gift of life?
Whatever we do, we must do it now.
Because we don't know when our last breath will be.
Breathe in and breathe out.
We have work to do.

Do You Know?

Hey, you, do you know
    that you are valued and loved
    that you are needed
    that you are precious?

Hey, do you know
Know that you are gifted
    that you are so talented
    that you are a game changer?

Hey, do you know
    that someone thinks you were to die for
    so much so he exchanged his life for yours
He took on your sins and problems so you can be the best person
    you can be?

Hey, do you know
    that you don't have to carry the heavy load alone
    that you don't have to live in guilt and shame
    that you can be whoever you want because God sees greatness
    in you?

Compass

God, show me the way
Point me in the right direction
Be my True North
Be my compass.

At times I feel like a child lost in the crowd
Trying to find the comfort of a parent's loving embrace
Hoping to hear it's going to be OK.
Other times I feel like a ship that has lost its way
Drifting in the current
Not knowing which way to steer my vessel to land.
Then at times it's like I'm stuck going through the motions
Day in and day out
Getting one job done and preparing for the next one.

In other words, I cannot move without guidance
I can't feel strong without your warm embrace
I need the shelter of your love
I need the hear the sirens of your calm still voice.
Lord, I need your light to shine brightly from the lighthouse
Your light to pierce through the darkness
To guide me to where I need to be.

God, show me the way
Point me in the right direction
Be my True North
Be my compass.

Autopilot

The world is on autopilot
It's just going through the motions
Millions and millions of people wandering aimlessly
They are hyper-focused on the current task
Then it's on to the next
Heads are glued to screens
They are oblivious to their surroundings
They can't see each other's hurt
They are unaware of chaos

Even in God's house
We see the same thing
We get caught up in doing the motions
Reciting prayers and singing hymns
We listen to the sermon and make a quick exit during the benediction
Where is the sacrifice?
Where is the service?
Where is the outreach and mission?

If we don't switch the autopilot off and allow ourselves to feel—
Allow ourselves to show emotions and empathy, allow ourselves to stand still and take in the beauty of this earth—
Then we are doomed to crash.
When we finally wake up it will be too late
It's time to let go of the yoke
And let God to guide us safely to our destination.

Faith

Faith is not just feeling good on Sunday.
It's not staying in your comfort zone.
It's not quitting because someone hurt your feelings.
It's hard work.
It's a daily struggle against fear and anxiety.
It's trusting in God no matter how bad it looks.
It requires sacrifice.
It's a leap into the unknown.
It restores.
It reshapes.
It heals.
It opens doors that were once closed.
It's the gift that can keep on giving.

The Sending Forth

Worship doesn't end when we all say, "Amen."
True worship starts when we leave the pews.
The real thing happens when we drive from the church grounds.
Do we apply what we learn?
Do we put our faith to the test?
Do we show love to everyone?
Do we have empathy and compassion?
God is not just exalted in worship and song.
He is praised when we do the work of helping each other.
He gets happy when we let our light shine.
The Sabbath is just the beginning.
When pastor says go in peace,
Those are our marching orders—
Our orders to share God's love.
The world needs to see God every day.
The world needs to see God in us.
The Sabbath is just the pre-game.
The real event happens when we all say, "Amen."
Are we ready to get in the game?

Mess

Here's the truth:
We are messy people
who judge people
whose mess is different from our mess.
Instead of cleaning up our own mess,
we spend time correcting other people's mess.
Then we dress up our mess so that the world sees us as fine.
We carry our mess that we don't resolve
into everything we do in the future.
So, we have a mess at work,
the mess in our homes,
and the mess in our places of worship.
We raise our kids in the same mess.
We try to minister to others in the same mess.
We teach others in the mess.
We spend our money and time trying to ignore and cover up our mess.
Then we wonder why this world is such a messy place.
God still loves us all despite of our mess.
He sent his son to pay the price of our mess.
His blood can clean any stain better than bleach and Dawn.
His Word provides comfort and guidance as we deal with our mess.
His Spirit gives us reassurance that we can be mess-free.
When we really take time and realize
that we are all a mess and stop judging each other,
we can work on cleaning up this world.

We can truly be the image of how God sees us ...
Diamonds in the rough shining bright and full of potential.
Imagine how much good we can do
If we can just let our mess go.

Whose Hands You're In

When all hope is lost
When there no way out
When it's life or death
Remember whose hands you're in

When you can't find the words
When you can't see your way through
When there seems to be no answer
Remember whose hands you're in

You're in the hands that created all you see
You're in the hands that painted the universe with stars and galaxies
You're in the hands that formed you in his image

You're in the hands that control the seasons
You're in the hands that make the impossible possible
You're in the hands that have performed miracles
You're in the hands that never make a mistake

You're in God's hands
Nothing today, tomorrow, or forever can harm you
Trust in the one who has you in his hands

With Every Drop

As he sits in the recliner with a warm blanket and his favorite
 shows on TV
The nurse comes and prepares him for chemo …
Anti-nausea medicine and a round
of the drug that will destroy the tumorous cells
that held him prisoner for
six months.
With every drop he's one step closer
Closer to being a survivor and no longer the patient
Closer to a new and better normal
With every drip he's closer
Closer to answered prayers
Closer to no longer being in a test and now having a testimony
Closer to being the victor and no longer a victim.
With every drop, God is guiding him to his healing.

He Carries Me

When the path gets dark
When the hill is too steep to climb
When I can't find my way
When every door is shut
When the tears seem to flow like a river
When it seems like I can't take another step

He carries me

When grief comes
When I don't know how to say goodbye
When the pain is too much to bear
When the load seems too heavy
When I don't understand
When it gets tough

He carries me

Being safe in his arms has made all the difference

One More

I got one more mountain to climb
Another river to cross
Lord, keep my soul steady
If not, I'll be lost

Another battery of tests
Another scan I must face
I'll do what I must
To get out of this place

I got one more mountain to climb
Another river to cross
Lord, keep my soul steady
If not, I'll be lost

Another step to routine is added
A new instrument to use
I'll do what I must
Giving up is something I refuse

I got one more mountain to climb
Another river to cross
Lord, steady my soul
If not, I'll be lost

This is just a setback
Just another test

I promise to give it my all
I'll give you my best

Because I have one more mountain to climb
Another river to cross
Lord, steady my soul
If not, I'll be lost

Faith over Fear

I'm so proud of him
Nothing seems to slow him down
Not surgery after surgery
Not chemo
Not even radiation
It's seeming like he has gotten more energized since he heard the word cancer
It's like he has a new lease on life
The thing that made me most proud
He gave all the credit to God
He inspired me
To search for the right gift
To keep his spirits up
I found it was a shirt with the words
"Faith Over Fear"
I rejoice and sing praises
Because I know if the timing was off by a few weeks
Dad could have been far worse
He's not the same man as he was six months ago
He's better despite it all
Because he chose his faith
And he ignored his fears

It's OK, Momma

It's OK, Momma, to take rest
You've done a great job
You gave it your best.

Don't stress yourself too much
Don't worry about me
Because of your love I'm always free.
Free to love
Free to help
Free to share God's love.

Take a load off, Momma
Take care of yourself
Remember good health is also wealth.
If the load gets too much
It's OK to let me carry
You need to relax
There's no need to hurry.

It's your golden years
It's time to relax a little and let our light shine
God will provide, Momma
We will be fine.

You taught me well
I say thanks for all you do
It's time that you let me take care of you.

Sick

I'm sick of hospitals
I'm sick of watching
I'm sick of waiting
I'm sick of the unanswered questions
I'm sick hearing alarms
I'm sick of checking vitals
I'm sick of being on edge
I'm sick of the what if's
I'm sick of the unknowns
I'm sick of being tired
I'm just sick of it all

The only cure
The only medication I have
Is faith
I trust God
I trust the doctors, nurses, aides, and techs
Because he created them
I trust the training and skills they have acquired to do their best
I trust that through it all God's will is done.
So, I'm going to take my medicine as prescribed
To trust in God and what his Word says
Healing is coming
Change is coming
Victory is coming
I just have to trust

The Fist Bump Part II

Once again, I touched fists with Dad
This time it wasn't an accomplishment
It wasn't a see you soon
This time it was goodbye
It was my closed fist to his tired open hand
He was tired and was ready to go home
I really thought you would come out of this one
I was planning your recovery
But you and God had other plans
Your healing was meant to be in heaven
So, this bump meant thank you
It meant the passing of the torch from father to son
It meant I would be the carrying the mantle
I knew when we touched hands,
I knew you were going to be with God
I knew that I no longer had to worry about you
Because you were on your way to shake Jesus's hand

When My Time Comes

When my time comes to live in my mansion in the sky
Remember me
Remember the first time we said hello
When I first said I love you
When I made you laugh until you cried
That even if we fought, we always found a compromise
Remember the trips we took
The fun we had
The times we faced adversity and overcame them
All we have accomplished
Remember how God kept us and answered our prayers
Remember how many storms he brought us through
Don't dwell on my passing
Don't linger in the sadness
See it as "I'll see you soon"
Most importantly, remember to live
Live your life to the fullest
And remember … God is not through with you yet.

My Dad, My Hero, My Friend

My dad, my hero, my friend …
Thanks for everything
For being my biggest fan
For being my protector
For being a provider
For correction
For your guidance
For loving me unconditionally
For making sure we wanted for nothing
Get your rest
You won your race
Victory is yours
I hope to see you again
My dad, my hero, my friend.

Three Pairs

Here lie three barely worn, brand-new pairs of shoes.
The owner transferred his residence to heaven.
They are mine now to do as I please.
I picked them out just for him.
He loved how they looked and felt.
The smile he had when he got them was priceless.
I wish I could see that smile again.
I sit and stare at them.
The man that wore these shoes had so much love in his heart.
He endured so much in such a short time.
I know he would want me to wear those brand-new shoes.
However, I hang my head in sorrow
Because I know I can never fill those shoes.
When God made him, he broke the mold.
I hope that one day I can fill those shoes.
I hope that one day I can fill those shoes.
God, grant me the strength to fill these shoes.

Another Restless Night

Sleep hasn't come easy
Here I am, replaying memories
Did this really happen?
Is he truly gone?
Did I receive the flag that draped his casket?
What could have I done differently?

I wish I could have said something
Through all the noise of my mind
I remember that I'm safe
I'm loved
And that these past things are not for me to ponder
It was his time to go home
His work was done
God gave him his peace
He is free from the pain.

I may not find rest tonight but
I can be assured that I'm going to be OK
For God is with me through it all.

No Worries

There is no need to worry
I will wipe your tears
I will help conquer your fears
I will always be near.

There is no need to worry
My love will help you endure
My Spirit will help you be pure
The strength I give is sure.

There is no need to worry
I will pick you up from the deep
I will protect you while you sleep
Trust me … a fruitful harvest you will reap.

I am the "I am"
I am the truth and the light
Keep your faith in me, my friends
You will be all right.

Six Stars

The service is over
The sun shines bright on the flag draped on his casket
Taps has been played
Ironically two U.S. carrier planes were flying above
Two soldiers in dress blues carefully fold the flag
It's perfect
No red shows
Only the stars
The sergeant kneels before me
She presents the flag in honor of Dad
On behalf of our president, country, and the U.S. Army
She thanks our family for my dad's honorable service
I take the flag and I see six stars looking at me
I can breathe now
The weight has been lifted
Dad made his last watch
Those hard-fought years in the jungles of Vietnam were not in vain
He didn't receive a hero's welcome when he got back
Somehow, I know he got a huge welcome home from God
He rejoiced to have his son back home
I look at those six stars every day and sometimes I smile
and others I shed a few tears
I rejoice in knowing that he's still standing guard
Watching over us.

There's No Road Map for Grief

There is no road map for grief
One day you are smiling
The next you find yourself crying
while making an appointment for an oil change.
One moment you are working constantly
then the next you don't want to be bothered.
On the outside, you are strong.
On the inside, you are fighting to keep it together .
It's like a weight that hits you out of the blue.
It's a rush of emotions.
No one grieves the same.
Some say time heals
Others say it's with them every day.
There's no right or wrong turn because everyone's journey is not
    the same
However, we have the same destination ...
Peace
The only way to reach that destination is to seek Jesus.
He's the compass that will guide us through the journey of tears
No there's no road map for this
All we can do is press forward
And hold firm to our faith.

A Letter to Dad

Dear Dad,
Nothing is the same since you left us.
We're left with a void in our hearts.
It's like the slightest memory can either make us laugh or cry.
Sometimes I even think I need to call you to tell you something
But I know you are not here.
The projects you had in mind are slowly getting done.
I wish we could've had a longer conversation
and I truly long for one more hug.
Every day I thank God for the privilege to have you as my dad.
Continue to get your rest.
You ran your race your way.
You made it to the finish line.
Don't worry, your spot is still intact under the garage.
The neighbors miss that wave and a smile.
If you don't mind, I may need to borrow your chair occasionally.
I'll sit in it and cherish the memories we had.
Your life lessons will be my road map.
Your legacy of faith has given me the strength to keep going.
Your smile will be forever in my heart.

I hope we meet again at the great coronation in the skies above,
From your loving son.

Cherish

Cherish the family trips
The car rides to the store
The long conversations about life and the good ole days.

Cherish the projects you've done together
The moments of joy when your favorite team wins
Cherish the holidays and family dinners
The days of just casting a line at our favorite spot with your best friend.

Cherish the firsts and the last moments
The tears of joy you see in your loved one's eyes
The opportunities to tell them that you loved them
The hugs and kisses
The slow dances.

Cherish the gentle breezes on a warm summer day
The colors of fall
The warmth of the fireplace
And the marvels of spring.

Cherish it all
Because we don't know when we must leave our earthly home for our heavenly one
We don't know when is the very last time
So, while you can
Just cherish the gift of life.

About the Author

Stephon Carlisle Void is a native of Bowman, South Carolina. An honors graduate of Bowman High School, he holds a Bachelor of Science in biology and a Master of Science in biotechnology from Claflin University of Orangeburg, South Carolina. He is the nuclear magnetic resonance technician in the Department of Chemistry at Claflin University and has been at Claflin for fourteen years.

Void is currently a certified lay servant in the South Carolina United Methodist Church at New Covenant UMC. He has served in this role for twenty years. He loves to serve his church and community in any way God needs him. He enjoys singing in the choir, community outreach, teaching Sunday school, and teaching the children and youth moment on Sundays.

Void developed a passion for writing when he was selected to participate as a contributing author for the latest African series for Discipleship Ministries of The United Methodist Church. His work appeared periodically throughout the 2020-2021 calendar year. His first book, *From My Heart to Your Eyes: Poems of Faith and Social Justice*, was published by the Advocate Press in 2021.

In his spare time, he writes a blog, "Stephon's Thoughts," at StephonCVoid.com, and enjoys spending time with family and friends. He resides with his mother, Shirlene Void, in Bowman.

For more writing from the author,
visit https://stephoncvoid.com

www.ingramcontent.com/pod-product-compliance
Lightning Source LLC
Chambersburg PA
CBHW032129090426
42743CB00007B/531